Disney's Year Book 2001

Disney's Year Book 2001

Published by Grolier Books

Grolier Books is a division of Grolier Enterprises, Inc.

FERN L. MAMBERG   *Executive Editor*
ELIZABETH A. DEBELLA   *Designer*
BARBARA L. PERSAN   *Production Manager*

ISBN: 0-7172-6491-2
ISSN: 0273-1274

Stories on pages 14-25, 34-45, 56-67, 76-87, and all Disney character artwork © 2001 Disney Enterprises, Inc.

Pages 14-25: Written by Barbara Bazaldua; based on the book *The One Hundred and One Dalmatians* by Dodie Smith, published by The Viking Press. Pages 34-45: Written by Amy Bauman. Pages 56-67: Written by Victoria Saxon. Pages 76-87: Written by Liane Onish. Page 96 (Eeyore art): Based on the Pooh stories by A. A. Milne, © The Pooh Properties Trust. Stories illustrated by Alvin S. White Studio.

Illustration Credits and Acknowledgments

6: © Ric Feld/AP/Wide World Photos; © Liu Qiangang/Xinhua/AP/Wide World Photos. 7: © Heather Angel. 8: Ron Garrison/San Diego Zoo/AP/Wide World Photos; © 1999 Zoological Society of San Diego. 9: © Joyce Naltchayan/AFP/Courtesy, Presslink. 10: © Dennis Cook/AP/Wide World Photos. 11: © Bettmann/Corbis. 12: © Jeff Tinsley/ Smithsonian Institution/AP/Wide World Photos. 26-27: From *Make Cards*! © 1992 by Kim Solga. Used with permission of North Light Books, a division of F&W Publications, Inc. 28: © Jerome Wexler/Photo Researchers, Inc. 29: © Melanie Stetson Freeman/*The Christian Science Monitor*. 30: © J.P. Thomas/Jacana/Photo Researchers, Inc.; 31: © Patti Murray/Animals Animals; © Hans Reinhard/ Bruce Coleman Inc.; © Claire Hayden/Tony Stone Images. 32: © Kathi Lamm/Tony Stone Images; © Fritz Prenzel/Animals Animals. 33: © Ulrike Schanz/Animals Animals; © Carolyn A. McKeone/ Photo Researchers, Inc. 46: Sam Ogden/ Science Photo Library/Photo Researchers, Inc. 47: © Hank Morgan/Science Source/Photo Researchers, Inc.; © David Parker/Science Photo Library/Photo Researchers, Inc.; NASA. 48: © Peter Menzel; 49: © Toshiyuki Aizawa/Reuters/Archive Photos. 50: © Renee Lynn/Photo Researchers, Inc. 51: © G.C. Kelley/Photo Researchers, Inc.; 52: Charles V. Angelo Photo Researchers, Inc.; © J. & D. Bartlett/Bruce Coleman, Inc. 53: © Jeff Lepore/Photo Researchers, Inc. 54: © Jeff Lepore/ Photo Researchers, Inc.; © Herb Segars/Animals Animals. 55: © Robert Winslow/Animals Animals. 68: © Toby Talbot/AP/Wide World Photos; Courtesy of the Archives of the American Illustrators Gallery, New York City. © 2000 by ASaP of Holderness, NH. 69: © Chris Gardner/AP/Wide World Photos; Courtesy of the Archives of the American Illustrators Gallery, New York City. © 2000 by ASaP of Holderness, NH. 70-71: The Granger Collection. 72: Bettmann/Corbis. 73: © Andrew J. Campbell/Mahopac Public Library. 74-75: Artist, Natasha Lessnik Tibbott. 88: © L. Newman & A. Flowers/Photo Researchers, Inc.; © Andrew J. Martinez/Photo Researchers, Inc. 88-89: © Gregory Ochocki/Photo Researchers, Inc. 89: © Steve Wolper/DRK Photo; © Fred Bavendam. 90: © Simon Battensby/Tony Stone Images; Reprinted with permission from AP Photo/© Science Magazine. © 1998 American Association for the Advancement of Science. 91: SuperStock. 92: © The Bata Shoe Museum; © Musee du Louvre, Paris/SuperStock. 93: © The Bata Shoe Museum. 94: © The Bata Shoe Museum; SuperStock. 95: © Myrleen Ferguson Cate/PhotoEdit.

 Contents

Panda Patrol

Giant pandas are the cutest! People of all ages love to watch these roly-poly animals. And in the year 2000, we had three new pandas to watch and love. It was PANDA-mania!

Lun-Lun and Yang-Yang are the new stars at Zoo Atlanta. Lots of people line up to see these cuddly cuties! Inset: Chinese wildlife officials are getting the pandas ready for their trip to America.

Giant pandas are very rare. There are only about 1,000 pandas in the world. More than 120 of those live in zoos and research centers. In the wild, giant pandas are found only in China.

Lucky panda lovers in Atlanta, Georgia, were thrilled in November 1999. That's when two giant pandas arrived at Zoo Atlanta. They came all the way from China on a special plane, the Panda Express.

The new pandas are Lun-Lun, a female, and Yang-Yang, a male. They are on loan from the Chinese government for ten years. Zoo Atlanta built a brand-new panda habitat for these very special animals.

Bamboo for Breakfast

Bamboo is the giant panda's favorite food. Pandas love to nibble tender bamboo shoots. In the wild, a panda can eat 85 pounds of bamboo in a day!

But many of China's bamboo forests have been cut. That means there's less food for wild pandas. And that's one reason why these wonderful animals are so rare.

In zoos, pandas eat other foods besides bamboo. They like rice, apples, carrots, cooked sweet potatoes, and cooked meat. But bamboo is what they like best!

Bai-Yun cuddles her baby, Hua-Mei, at the San Diego Zoo. Inset: Hua-Mei weighed about 8 pounds when this picture was snapped. She'll weigh nearly 300 pounds when she grows up!

Panda fans in California had lots to cheer about, too. A tiny female panda cub was born at the San Diego Zoo on August 21, 1999. The cub's parents were Shi-Shi, a male, and Bai-Yun, a female. Both live at the zoo.

Pandas born in zoos often don't live long. But Bai-Yun took excellent care of her baby. Her cub was the first panda born in the United States to survive.

The cub was named Hua-Mei. In Chinese, that name has two meanings: "splendid beauty" and "China USA." Zoo visitors had their first look at Hua-Mei in February 2000. The cuddly baby was almost six months old.

April 2000 brought more good news for panda lovers. The National Zoo, in Washington, D.C., announced that its Giant Panda House would soon have new tenants.

The Giant Panda House was built for two pandas that China gave to the United States in 1972. Hsing-Hsing and Ling-Ling were the National Zoo's top stars for many years. But Ling-Ling died in 1992. And Hsing-Hsing died in 1999. They were greatly missed.

Visitors to the National Zoo, in Washington, D.C., miss Hsing-Hsing. The popular giant panda died in 1999. But the zoo hopes to have new pandas soon.

Now the National Zoo plans to bring two new pandas from China. The zoo expects thousands of visitors to line up for a close look at the new pandas when they arrive. Cute, playful pandas always draw big crowds!

Before work started on the star-spangled banner, it hung in Flag Hall, in the Smithsonian's National Museum of American History.

Oh, Say Can You See...

"Oh, say can you see, by the dawn's early light. . ." These are the first words of "The Star-Spangled Banner," the national anthem of the United States. The song was named after a real star-spangled banner—a giant flag that's almost 200 years old. This famous flag has been a top attraction at the

Smithsonian Institution in Washington, D.C., for many years. But it was in danger of falling apart. So experts are working to fix and preserve it.

The story of the star-spangled banner and the writing of the national anthem are an important part of American history. During the War of 1812, the flag flew over Fort McHenry, in Baltimore Harbor. British warships attacked the fort on September 13, 1814. From a ship near the harbor, an American lawyer named Francis Scott Key watched the attack.

British cannons bombarded the fort all night. But in the morning, "by the dawn's early light," Key saw that the flag was still flying over the fort. The British attack had failed! Key was so glad that he quickly wrote a poem. Later, his words were

"By the dawn's early light," Francis Scott Key saw "that our flag was still there." And he wrote the words to "The Star-Spangled Banner."

Star-Spangled Facts

★ The flag that inspired "The Star-Spangled Banner" was made in 1813 by Mary Pickersgill of Philadelphia and her 13-year-old daughter, Caroline.

★ The flag that they made was huge. It was one quarter the size of a basketball court!

★ The flag has 15 stripes and 15 stars—one stripe and one star for each state in the Union at that time.

★ One of the stars and other parts of the flag were cut away and given to people as mementos.

set to music. And that song, "The Star-Spangled Banner," became the national anthem.

The tattered flag that survived that night became more tattered over the years. Even after the flag was placed in the Smithsonian Institution in 1907, its condition continued

Workers begin to repair the star-spangled banner. Visitors to the Smithsonian can watch them from a special room.

The Star-Spangled Banner

Words by Francis Scott Key

Music by John Stafford Smith

O— say! can you see, by the dawn's ear - ly light, What so proud - ly we hailed at the twi - light's last gleam - ing? Whose broad stripes and bright stars, through the per - il - ous fight, O'er the ram - parts we watch'd, were so gal - lant - ly stream - ing! And the rock - ets' red glare, the bombs burst - ing in air, Gave proof through the night that our flag was still there. O say, does that___ Star - Span - gled Ban - ner___ yet___ wave___ O'er the land___ of the free and the home of the brave?

to get worse. Finally, in late 1998, the flag was taken down to be fixed. Visitors to the Smithsonian can watch the work from a special observation room.

When the historic flag is repaired, it will go back on view. Then it will be ready to inspire new generations of Americans.

A Scarecrow for Roger

One sunny spring morning, Roger marched into the backyard of the new Dalmatian plantation. He was wearing a big straw hat and carrying a shovel, a rake, a hoe, and a basket filled with seed packages, string, and planting sticks.

"I'm going to plant the biggest, greenest vegetable garden in all England!" he announced to the puppies who were following him. "Just think, Patch—all the peas you can eat! Lucky shall have lots of lettuce. And Rolly—why, you'll be munching deeeeelicious radishes from now till Christmas!"

The puppies made faces behind Roger's back.

14

"EEEyuck!" Rolly whispered. "Radishes don't sound 'deeeeelicious' to me! Why doesn't he plant dog biscuits?"

Roger measured out the space for the garden. Then he began to dig.

"Let's help Roger!" Patch barked to the other puppies. They all began digging. Dirt and rocks flew through the air. A pebble bounced off Roger's head. "Whoa there, pups!" Roger said, rubbing his head and looking at the hole the puppies had dug. "We aren't digging a swimming pool. Better let me do it."

The puppies sat down in the shade of a tree

and watched Roger finish digging. Then he smoothed the earth. Next, he began putting sticks into the ground and tying string from one stick to another.

"Roger must want to play fetch," Lucky said to Penny. "Let's show him how good we are at fetching sticks." Penny and Lucky bounded into the garden, pulled up all the sticks and strings, and ran to Roger. Around and around his legs they ran, until his feet were completely tangled. Over he went, in a heap of puppies, sticks, and strings.

"No, no, puppies," Roger said as he untangled himself. "We're not playing fetch today. Those sticks are to help me make straight rows for the seeds. Now, go sit down."

Once again, the pups trotted over to their shady spot and plopped down to watch.

"Look at Roger now!" Penny exclaimed. "He's burying something in the ground."

"Bones!" Rolly barked. "I bet he's burying bones." With a hungry little bark, Rolly followed Roger, digging up every hole that Roger had covered with dirt. But all he dug up were little round brown seeds. Rolly tasted a couple.

"Phooey!" He spit them out. "Whatever these are, they taste AWFUL!" he informed his brothers and sisters. "I hope they aren't radishes!"

Roger heard Rolly barking and turned around. Then he saw the holes. "Oh, gracious, puppies!" Roger exclaimed. "How will my garden grow with you digging? I'll have to find something

for you to do." He thought a moment. Then he gathered the puppies around him. He took a stick and drew a picture of a bird in the dirt.

"Now, this is a crow," he told them. "Crows eat up all the seeds, so nothing can grow. I want you to watch the garden and chase off any crows you see. Can you do that?"

The puppies nodded their heads.

Roger drew another picture. "This is a rabbit," he said. "They eat up all the plants. When you see one, I want you to bark loudly and chase it away. Can you do that?"

Once again, the puppies nodded.

So every day the puppies watched Roger's garden. They barked at the crows and scampered after the rabbits. At last, little green plants appeared in rows and began to grow taller and taller.

"Look how well my garden is growing," Roger said proudly. "You are excellent watch puppies!"

But what no one knew was that while the puppies were watching the garden every day, someone was watching them. Cruella De Vil had followed the puppies to the Dalmatian plantation. Now she was standing in the woods, disguised in a long black coat and a big black hat.

"I'm not finished with those puppies yet," she muttered, swinging a long tan sack—just the right size to hold a couple of pups. "I'll watch and wait and wait and watch. Sooner or later, Roger and Anita will leave the plantation, and I'll nab them."

That very afternoon, Roger and Anita went shopping. Cruella watched them drive away. "Now's my chance!" she sniggered, creeping toward the garden.

Just as Cruella was sneaking up, Rolly spotted a rabbit.
"Woof! Scoot! Scram!" he barked, racing toward the little
rabbit. The other puppies joined in, chasing the rabbit up and
down the rows of vegetables. Then, suddenly, they heard a
high cackling laugh. The puppies froze. There stood Cruella,
her long black coat flapping around her like huge wings.

"It's a GIANT CROW!" Rolly yelped.

"That's not a crow, it's CRUELLA!" Patch barked. "Run!"

Around and around the
garden the puppies raced,
with Cruella after them. The
confused little
rabbit ran this
way and that,
looking for a
way out. Finally,

with a frightened squeak, it dashed between Cruella's feet.
PLOP! Down went Cruella. CLUNK! Down fell her long tan
sack. SPLAT! Off flew her boots. WHOOSH! Away flew her
big black hat. Cruella's fall gave the puppies the time they
needed.

"Dig! Dig! Dig a hole!" Rolly barked.

"Oof! Uhh! Yaah!" Cruella shouted as pebbles and mud
splatted, thunked, and plunked onto her head. "I'll get you
yet!" she shouted, stumbling
between the rows of cabbages
and carrots.

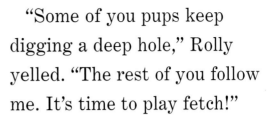

"Some of you pups keep digging a deep hole," Rolly yelled. "The rest of you follow me. It's time to play fetch!"

Rolly raced for the sticks and strings and yanked them up. The other puppies followed him. Around and around they ran, winding the sticks and strings around Cruella's legs. Soon she was so tangled, she could barely move. As she yanked at the sticks and strings, her coat fell into the lettuce patch.

"You wretched dogs!" she screamed, lunging for Lucky. At that moment, the little rabbit dashed between her legs again. KER-PLUNK!

Cruella fell right into the very deep, very muddy hole that the puppies had dug.

"AAAAH!" she screamed as she went down. "ARRRGH!" she snarled as she struggled up, covered with mud.

Just then, Roger and Anita returned from town. "What's going on?" Roger shouted. Cruella turned and hopped out of the garden, across the field, and into the trees.

"Oh, my! Look at my poor garden," Roger said with a sigh. Then he looked at the puppies and smiled. "And look at all of you," he said. "You're all safe and sound, and that's what really counts."

Lucky trotted over, dragging Cruella's hat. Patch and Penny came carrying her boots and her long tan sack. And Rolly

dropped Cruella's long black coat at Roger's feet.

Roger looked at the clothes and began to laugh. "You're very good watch puppies," he said, "but now you'll have a little help. Let's use Cruella's long black coat and big black hat to make a scarecrow. We'll put her black boots on its feet, and hang her long tan sack on its arm. What do you think of that?"

The puppies barked with glee. From then on, no crows or rabbits came anywhere near the garden. And soon Roger had the biggest, greenest garden in all England.

But Rolly never did learn to like radishes.

Use bits of candies and cookies, some coins, and a bunch of straw to make these wild cards! Or create your own cards with other "leftovers" you find around the house.

You can work with pictures from old magazines, scraps of cloth, and bits of colored paper.

Half the fun of making these cards is looking for stuff to make them with!

1. To make this **Candy Card**, arrange small candies on a graham cracker so they make a picture.

2. Make frosting "glue" by stirring a teaspoon of milk or water into 1/4 cup of powdered sugar.

3. One at a time, lift the candies off the cracker. Dip the bottom into the frosting. Set them back in place. Let dry.

Use pennies, nickels, and dimes to create this fishy coin card. It would make a great "Good Luck" card.

1. To make this **Straw Card**, cut a rectangle shape from cardboard. Paint it with black acrylic paint. Let the paint dry.

2. Cut the straw into strips. Glue these onto the black cardboard to create a picture. Let the glue dry completely.

3. Glue your picture onto the front of a folded card that's a little bigger than your picture.

CRAZY ABOUT CATS

Cats are MEOW-velous. They are the PURR-fect pets. No wonder millions of these furry felines are living happily in homes everywhere. But just because cats live in your home, don't think that you own them. Most cat lovers say that their cats own them! And cats, who are very independent, seem to agree.

Cats are not only independent, they're intelligent, too. And they're tidy. Best of all, they are amusing.

Cats can be amusing even when they're sleeping. They'll sleep anywhere—on top of a tall bookcase, in a box, or on your lap. And they'll sleep in any number of peculiar positions—on their back, curled up in a ball, or with their paws cradling their head. Cats just love to sleep. In fact, a cat can sleep as much as 17 hours a day.

When cats aren't sleeping, they spend a great deal of time grooming—about 3½ hours a day. A cat keeps clean by licking itself all over with its rough tongue. The

SIT, KITTY

Want to train your cat to sit whenever you tell it to? Try this: Move a spoonful of cat food up over its head. Say "sit" as you do. As the spoon moves overhead, your cat will look up to follow it. At the same time, the cat will automatically sit. (If it doesn't, *gently* press its hind end down.) When the cat sits, say "good sit," and reward it with a bit of the food.

Do this many times. Your cat will soon make the connection between your command, the action of sitting, and getting food. When that happens, the cat will sit when you tell it to. Although, with independent-minded cats, you can't really be sure of that!

BLACK CATS

Is it bad luck for a black cat to cross your path? That's an old superstition—a belief that isn't based on fact.

The idea that black cats bring bad luck goes back hundreds of years. That's when people thought that black cats were actually evil witches in disguise.

But not everybody believed that. Long ago in China, black cats were thought to bring good luck. And in Britain today, many people consider a black cat to be a good-luck charm.

tongue whisks away dirt and loose hairs. Cats seem to like cleanliness so much that some even groom their owners!

Clawing is another natural cat activity. Cats are obeying their instinct to stretch their claws and mark their territory. It's best to provide a scratching post so your cat won't wreck all the furniture.

Cats also "knead" soft objects—such as a pillow or your lap—by pressing with their paws over and over again. Kittens do these "paw presses" while they nurse. This helps the mother's milk to flow. When adult cats knead, it usually means they're content.

What does a cat do all day? It sleeps most of the time. It also spends time cleaning itself. And sometimes it waits silently for just the right moment to pounce on a mouse—and bring it to you as a token of affection.

Cats are also known for their "cat chat." They make lots of different sounds. They meow. They mew. They hiss. They yowl. The sound that cat owners love best, though, is the rumbling, humming sound of a cat's purr. Kittens as young as one week

old purr while they nurse. And cats of all ages make this noise when they're content. But cats also purr when they aren't feeling well or when they're injured.

How can you tell whether your cat is content or ill? Here are some clues:

- Are your cat's ears perked up, and its tail relaxed? The cat is probably happy and relaxed.
- Are the ears flat back? The cat may be frightened.
- Is the tail held high, with the tip flicking back and forth? The cat may feel threatened.
- When a cat feels really threatened, it may even strike a "Halloween pose." It arches its back and puffs out the fur on its back and tail. The pose makes the cat look bigger than it actually is. And this may scare off an enemy.

The most popular cat breeds include the fluffy, longhaired Persian (opposite page, left); the graceful, blue-eyed Siamese (opposite page, right); the fabulous Maine coon cat (above); and the unusual lop-eared Scottish fold (right).

When your cat is especially content, it may run to greet you and rub its head against your legs. You may think it's showing affection. In fact, the cat is saying, "You're mine, all mine!" The cat has scent glands on its head. As it presses against you, some of the scent rubs off on your body. You won't notice it, but other cats will. And they'll know that you "belong" to your cat!

It's hard not to be charmed by these graceful and delightful creatures.

Birds of a Feather

Cinderella had always been kind to animals. As a girl, she had helped her father feed the barnyard animals and spread seed for the songbirds and mice. It had been fun for them both.

Unfortunately, when Cinderella's father died, many things changed. Her stepmother seemed to find a new way to be unkind each day. So it was no surprise when Lady Tremaine sternly called Cinderella into the parlor and made a cruel announcement.

34

"We will be making some changes around here," Cinderella's stepmother said. "There will be no more handouts from this house."

"What do you mean?" Cinderella asked.

"I mean," her stepmother answered, "that there will be no more free food for creatures who give nothing in return. Everyone in this household will earn his or her keep!"

"Oh, no, Stepmother!" Cinderella cried. "It may seem that the animals don't do anything to earn the food we give them, but that's not true. They are all useful to us."

Lady Tremaine smiled. "You can explain that to me tonight. I'll decide then which animals will eat . . . and which will not." She waved Cinderella away. "Now, get back to your chores."

Cinderella sat down on the soft hay in the barnyard. Bruno
the dog, the songbirds, the mice, and the chickens all gathered
around the horse's stall. "I know you're all important here,"
she said to them. "I just have to make Stepmother see it."

Sadly, Cinderella couldn't do that. The horse, Lady Tremaine
could see, was needed to pull the carriage and the plow; the
chickens supplied eggs. Bruno, she agreed, did serve as a
watchdog. But with the songbirds and the mice, she stood firm.
"The wild birds and mice do nothing for us," she declared. "I
can't keep them from nesting here, but, as I said before, there
will be no more handouts from this house!"

In the days that followed, the estate grew quiet. The songbirds visited now and then, but they were usually too busy looking for their next meal. Even the mice weren't around much, and when they were, they were exhausted from their daily search for food.

Cinderella wasn't the only one who noticed that the little animals were gone. A sneaky pair of magpies found out and began using the songbirds' nest. They weren't looking for food, so Lady Tremaine didn't object . . . at first. But they were very loud and bothersome—chasing the chickens, annoying the horse, and upsetting Bruno. Sometimes Cinderella would catch them at a window, peering inside. And more than once, she heard Drizella or Anastasia shooing the magpies away from the tree in front of the house.

Cinderella knew the magpies were up to no good. She was thinking about that one morning as she searched for her sewing thimble. Suddenly she heard her name screeched.

"Cinderella! Where are my earrings?" shouted Drizella.

"And I'm missing a bracelet!" Anastasia whined. "Something is going on around here." She squinted at Cinderella.

Just then, the three girls heard a scream. Lady Tremaine rushed into the room.

"Stepmother! What's wrong?" Cinderella cried.

"My necklace!" her stepmother shouted. "It's gone!" As she spoke, she was opening drawers and searching shelves.

As Lady Tremaine paced, the magpies landed on the windowsill. "I wore it yesterday," she said above their chattering. "Anastasia, Drizella, help me find my necklace." Then she turned to Cinderella. "And you, Cinderella. Get rid of those awful birds."

"Gladly, Stepmother . . . but how?" Cinderella asked.

"I don't care how you do it!" her stepmother shrieked, waving her hands. "Find some help—maybe those useless birds and mice you used to feed. Just get rid of those awful, noisy creatures!"

Cinderella brightened. It was as if her stepmother had forgotten she had banished the songbirds and mice. Maybe, if they could help her get rid of the magpies, she could prove that they were useful to the estate.

It didn't take long for Cinderella to gather the birds and mice. It took even less time to enlist their help. But getting rid of the magpies was another matter. They needed a plan.

"Maybe we can figure out a way to scare the magpies away," Cinderella mused. "After all, every animal is afraid of something." She turned and saw Lucifer curled up on his velvet pillow. "And every animal has a use." She laughed. "Even Lucifer."

The mice and birds looked doubtful.

"I know he won't help us willingly, but he's our only chance!" Cinderella said. "Follow me, everyone, but be careful not to wake the cat."

Under Cinderella's instruction, the mice carefully tied a harness of ribbon around Lucifer's pillow. Then, gingerly, the birds struggled to lift him into the air, carrying him up to where the magpies were napping.

"Lower Lucifer in front of their nest," Cinderella told the little birds. "When the magpies wake up, the sight of a cat should scare those pests away for good.

"We'll have Lucifer back on the ground before he even knows what's up!"

It would have worked as planned if Lucifer hadn't awakened too soon. Spotting the ground far below, he let loose a yowl. The magpies awoke to see Lucifer—all claws and fangs—nearly on top of them.

As the magpies flew off, the little songbirds fluttered quickly to earth. When Lucifer's feet hit solid ground, he took off running. He wasn't aware of the birds, the mice, Cinderella, or the role he had played in their plan.

"Well, that wasn't so bad," Cinderella laughed as she watched the magpies fly out of sight. She turned to see the songbirds swooping excitedly in and out of their nest. "Now what's bothering them?" she wondered.

That night, Cinderella waited until the supper dishes were cleared to tell her stepmother of the day's events.

"Stepmother," she said simply, "the magpies are gone."

Lady Tremaine glanced up. "Good."

"And when the songbirds reclaimed their nest, they found a few interesting items," Cinderella said. She held out her hands. In them were Anastasia's bracelet, Drizella's earrings, Cinderella's thimble, and . . .

"My necklace!" exclaimed her stepmother, snatching it from Cinderella.

Cinderella smiled, saying, "Thanks to the mice and birds, we won't be 'losing' anything else. I guess they've earned their keep . . . right, Stepmother?"

"Very well," her stepmother answered without looking up. "Very well."

Drizella and Anastasia glared at Cinderella. They didn't like the fact that Cinderella had proved her point. But if they argued with their mother, Cinderella didn't hear. By that time, she was halfway into the barnyard with a feast for all the animals to share.

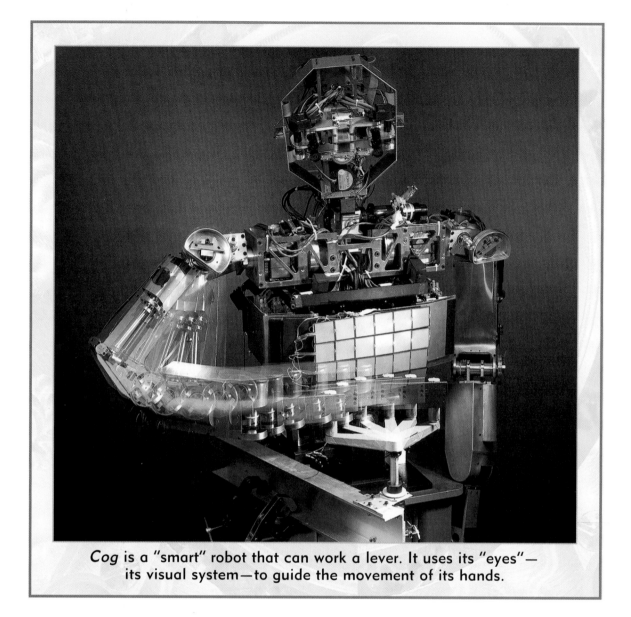

Cog is a "smart" robot that can work a lever. It uses its "eyes"—
its visual system—to guide the movement of its hands.

"SMART" ROBOTS

Do you dislike making your bed? Washing the dishes?
Cleaning your room? Walking the dog? Well, one day you may
have a personal robot to take care of these chores!

Robots are already doing lots of work for people. They do
some boring factory jobs, like bolting parts in place on cars.

This kind of robot is really just a giant arm. It's programmed to do just one thing.

There are more complex robots. These robots explore places where people can't go. They scout the bottom of the ocean. They explore the craters of active volcanoes. One robot, named *Sojourner*, has even explored parts of Mars. These robots also do dangerous jobs, like checking out poisonous oil spills.

But what about a personal robot that will do your chores?

Robots at work: A factory robot (right) attaches auto parts, over and over again. *Dante II* (below) explores volcanoes and other areas where people can't go. *Sojourner* (below right) tries to find out what the soil and rocks on Mars are made of.

Kismet is a robot that can show lots of different "moods." It does this by changing its eyes, eyebrows, mouth, and ears. Here, it shows surprise (top), anger (center), and sleepiness (bottom).

Suppose, for example, you want your robot to go to the kitchen and get you a banana. It would need to understand your command. It would have to get into the kitchen without banging into furniture. It would have to find and recognize bananas. It would have to pick one up without squashing it. And then it would have to find its way back to you.

Today's robots can't do this. That's because it's very hard to build a machine that can copy human actions and intelligence. But robots are getting better and smarter all the time. They have more powerful computers for "brains." They have sensors that let them "see" and "hear." They have software that allows them to "understand" commands. And they have lots of other new and amazing features.

Some robots, for example, can walk, wave, bow, shake hands, pick up objects, and go up and down stairs. Experts are working on robots that can perform even harder tasks. One experimental robot named *Cog* can learn new tasks like playing the drums. It can also make decisions and learn from

PUPPY LOVE

It walks like a dog. It barks like a dog. But it's definitely not a dog! It's AIBO—a plastic robot that looks like a pet puppy. AIBO is about the size of a Chihuahua. And it can walk, sit, beg, stretch, yawn, raise a paw, and dance a little hula. If you pat AIBO on its head, it wags its tail. The robot puppy even flashes its eyes green when it's happy and red when it's unhappy.

its mistakes. *Kismet*, another new robot, is programmed to have "moods," which it shows in "facial expressions." If you talk to *Kismet*, it smiles!

These robots seem almost human. And in as little as 30 years, some experts say, robots will be able to "think" like people. Maybe then you will have a personal "bot" at your beck and call. And then you won't have to clean your room anymore!

Animal Tails

Animals use their tails to do many things. Sending messages is one of the most important. When a skunk raises its bushy tail, take cover!

Short or long, simple or fancy, animal tails are important. Some animals can't get along without them. Tails are used for flying, sitting, eating, and hunting. The animals shown on these pages use their tails to scare an enemy, get a mate, swim, run, jump, fight—and even store food!

A skunk uses its tail to keep enemies away. If you see a skunk lower its head and lift its black-and-white tail like a battle flag, watch out! It means that the skunk is getting ready to fire. If you don't get away fast, the skunk will twist into a U-shaped position, aim its head and tail at you, and let go with its smelly spray. Phew!

Birds often use their tails for another reason—to attract mates. That's why some male birds, like the peacock, have large colorful tail feathers called a train. The peacock opens his train by shaking himself. His dazzling feathers rise behind him and spread out like a lacy fan. Then he struts about, turning around slowly as the peahens watch.

What a show-off! Male peacocks have large, colorful tail feathers that they use to attract a female.

Like most fish, this fairy basslet uses its tail as a propeller to glide in the water.

Some fish also have beautiful tails. But whether the tail is plain or pretty, a fish would be helpless without it. That's because a fish uses its tail as a propeller, to move around. It swims by twisting its body and beating its tail fin from side to side.

A kangaroo needs its long tail to balance the weight of its body as it bounds through the air.

With its strong grasping tail, the opossum can easily dangle upside down from a tree branch.

On the ground, tails help many animals keep their balance as they run and jump. A kangaroo is a powerful jumper. It can cover 30 feet with a single bound. It uses its outstretched tail to balance the weight of its body as it leaps through the air. Without its tail, the kangaroo would topple over when it tried to jump.

Many animals that live in trees have special tails that can grasp a limb or branch and hang on. The tail is like a long, skinny arm with one strong finger at the end, instead of a hand. It helps the animal climb about in the treetops. An opossum, for example, uses its tail as a safety belt when it hangs upside down from branches. The opossum anchors its tail to one end of a branch while reaching with its paws for ripe fruit at the other end.

Few animals are foolish enough to attack a porcupine. A porcupine has thousands of sharp quills buried under its long

fur. Lots of those quills are in its tail. If a porcupine is threatened, it turns its back to the enemy and lashes out with its tail. A single slap of that tail can drive hundreds of quills into the enemy. That hurts! After attacking a porcupine once, most animals learn their lesson. They never try it again.

In the sea, stingrays have tails that are like whips. And the tails have long, poisonous spines that are very sharp. When a stingray is disturbed, it

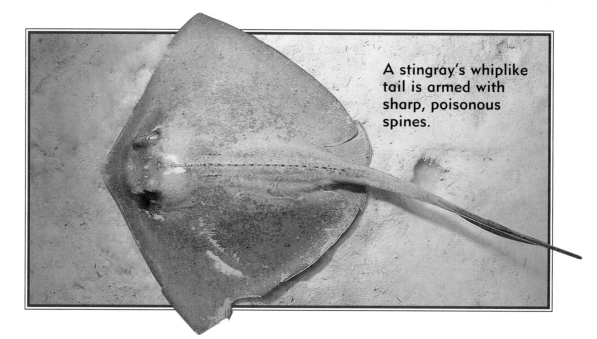

A stingray's whiplike tail is armed with sharp, poisonous spines.

snaps its tail from side to side or over its head. If an enemy is nearby, the sharp spines can seriously hurt it.

A lizard called the Gila monster can store food in its tail! Gila monsters live in desert regions. There's not a lot of food there.

The Gila monster stores fat in its tail, just as a camel stores fat in its hump.

So when these animals have a chance, they eat more than they need. The extra food is changed to fat and stored in the Gila monster's tail for future use—just as a camel stores body fat in its hump.

For many animals, the tail is an important part of their body. Without it, they couldn't survive.

Mowgli Finds His Place

Mowgli stretched slowly in the warm sunlight. He had slept well among the roots of a huge old tree. The day before, he had run away from the Man-village.

"Woo-hooo!" he cried, leaping up from his bed of leaves. It sure felt great to be back in the jungle!

Suddenly Mowgli stopped in his tracks. Stretching down from the tree was the sneaky snake, Kaa.

"You mussst be very sssleepy," Kaa said, his eyeballs
whirling. Mowgli slipped quickly under Kaa's spell.

Just then Bagheera the panther crept down from a boulder.
"Leave the boy alone!" Bagheera commanded. Startled, the
snake lost his balance and fell to the ground. When he landed,
he found his tail tied in a knot!

As Kaa creaked away, Bagheera turned back toward Mowgli
and licked his face.

"What?" Mowgli mumbled as he began to focus on the black cat in front of him. "What happened?"

"You were hypnotized by that snake, Kaa," Bagheera explained. "Luckily I remembered a trick of yours and managed to make him tie himself into a knot!"

"Bagheera!" Mowgli said, fully alert now. "Boy, am I glad to see you!"

"I'm glad to see you, too, my boy!" Bagheera replied. "But what are you doing back in the jungle?"

"I decided to come home," Mowgli announced.

"But whatever for?" Bagheera asked. "You belong in the Man-village. That's your home now."

"No, it's not!" Mowgli replied bitterly. "I don't fit in with them. I don't know any of their silly games. I don't like the taste of their food. And I can't understand their language. I just don't belong, Bagheera. Please let me come home," he pleaded. "Take me to Rama and my wolf family."

"Very well," Bagheera replied. "I'll take you back for a short visit, but that's all. Now hop up on my back."

Mowgli and his wise old teacher began the journey toward the home of his wolf family. "He'll find his place in the Man-village sooner or later," Bagheera told himself as he padded through the jungle.

"Bagheera," Mowgli said after a while, "I've been thinking. Maybe you could teach me to be a panther. Then I could stay with you in the jungle where I belong."

"You are a Man-cub, Mowgli," Bagheera said. "I can't—"

"Please?" Mowgli begged. "I'll do everything you tell me. We could at least try, couldn't we?"

"Very well," Bagheera said at last. "We'll try. Now hop down. I want to climb that tree over there to get a better view of where we are."

Mowgli jumped off Bagheera's back and watched as his friend dug his claws into the tree and climbed its trunk.

"I'll show him," Mowgli thought with great determination.

But when he tried to climb the tree trunk, Mowgli's hands slipped helplessly. Bagheera had to jump back down from the tree and give the boy a push. Then when Mowgli tried to jump from one branch to another, he slipped and tumbled onto the soft soil below the tree.

"I'll never be a panther!" Mowgli said angrily. He grabbed a fistful of dirt and threw it on the ground. "I don't have claws, and my legs aren't strong enough!"

Bagheera sighed. "Don't worry, Mowgli," he said. "We're almost at Rama's den. You'll have a nice visit with him. Then you can return to the Man-village."

"Or," Mowgli said, "I can learn to be a wolf!"

But when Mowgli was staying with Rama and the rest of his wolf family, he found that he wasn't one of them either. He was cold at night because he didn't have fur, and he was ashamed that his teeth weren't sharp enough to eat their food.

"We love you as our son," Rama said gently. "You don't need to be a wolf. But I'm afraid you can't live with us in the jungle. It's too dangerous for a Man-cub."

Later that morning Mowgli overheard Bagheera talking to Rama. The panther agreed he would take Mowgli back to the Man-village.

Mowgli just knew he'd be miserable and unhappy in the Man-village. So he sneaked away into the jungle when no one was looking. He ran until he came to a stream, where he flopped down on the mossy bank and started to cry.

"Why all the tears, buddy?" a voice interrupted him.

"Because I don't belong anywhere!" Mowgli wailed.

"Well, I think you look fine right where you are," the voice said gently.

Mowgli looked up then and saw a great big, happy-looking bear sitting next to him. "Baloo!" Mowgli cried happily. "Where did you come from?"

"Well, when I heard you were back in the jungle, I had to come and welcome you, Little Britches."

"Baloo," Mowgli asked, "would you teach me to be a bear, so I can live here with you?"

"Aw, kid, why would you want to live like a bear?"

"Because I don't feel like I belong anywhere!" Mowgli complained. "I don't understand the ways of the Man-village; and I'm not a good panther or wolf. I don't have claws or sharp teeth or fur or strong legs!"

"Slow down, kid," Baloo said. "I got an idea."

Baloo led Mowgli toward a grove of banana trees. As they walked along, they sang happily.

Suddenly Baloo stopped. "Hey, kid," he said, "I'll race you to that banana tree!"

"You're on!" Mowgli cried. Then he raced ahead of his friend and easily won the race.

"Good job, Little Britches," Baloo said. "Now, can you give me a hand reaching some of those bananas? I'll lift you up, and you grab a bunch."

"Sure, Baloo," Mowgli said. He scrambled up on Baloo's shoulders and plucked several bananas. Then the two friends settled down for lunch.

"Well, Mowgli, what do you

think?" Baloo finally asked. "Do you really still think you don't fit in anywhere?"

Mowgli thought quietly for a moment.

"I'll tell you what I think," Baloo said. "I think your long legs help you run fast, and your hands may not have claws, but they're sure good at picking fruit. Your teeth are fine for chewing bananas. And you're about as much fun to be with as anybody I know. See, kid? You're perfect just the way you are."

Mowgli smiled. "I guess I could learn to talk to the other Man-cubs. They

would probably teach me
their games, too. And maybe I can
teach them about my jungle friends. Then
maybe I would fit in with them better."

"I bet you could," Baloo said.

Early the next morning, Baloo walked with Mowgli to the
edge of the Man-village.

"Baloo," Mowgli said as he turned to say good-bye, "can I still come back and visit you?"

"You can go wherever you want, kid," Baloo replied. "Now go show 'em what ya got!"

And with that, Mowgli headed to the village. He knew he could fit in just fine.

PAINTING
Small-Town Life

Children on their way to school. A family sitting down to Thanksgiving dinner. A group of teens chatting at the drugstore soda fountain.

An artist named Norman Rockwell painted scenes like these. He created most of his works from the 1920's through the 1970's.

The Babysitter shows that there are some jobs that just can't be done by reading a book! In 1946, Norman Rockwell gave this painting to a 6th-grade class in Vermont.

This 1950 painting is called *Boy Practicing Trumpet.* Do you think the look on the dog's face tells what the music sounds like?

Over the years, Rockwell has become one of the best-loved American artists of all time. People enjoy his paintings because they show small-town life at its best. His pictures are heartwarming and often funny. And Rockwell had a wonderful talent for capturing facial expressions.

Now a special show is bringing Rockwell's works to some of the top museums in the United States. The name of the show is "Norman Rockwell: Paintings for the People." It will continue to tour through 2001.

Before there was indoor plumbing, kids took baths in washtubs. In *Lickin' Good Bath*, the family dog tries to "help." Old-fashioned, funny scenes like this made Rockwell famous.

Vacation Time shows a boy at his desk in school. He's holding a book, but he's dreaming about fishing and summer vacation fun.

The show is a wonderful treat for the millions of people who have always loved his paintings—and for the people who will see his work for the first time.

On these pages are some of Norman Rockwell's paintings of life in small-town America many years ago.

Paul Revere's Ride

Listen my children, and you shall hear
Of the midnight ride of Paul Revere,
On the eighteenth of April, in Seventy-five;
Hardly a man is now alive
Who remembers that famous day and year.

HENRY WADSWORTH LONGFELLOW

These words are the beginning of a famous poem called "Paul Revere's Ride." The poem tells of a great American patriot and his historic midnight ride more than 200 years ago.

Paul Revere was a silversmith in Boston, Massachusetts. In the years before the American Revolution, he and other colonists were unhappy with British rule. The colonists said that the British had no right to tax them without their consent. They also wanted the right to form their own government.

In 1773, the colonists were angry because the British had placed a new tax on tea. So Revere and 100 other Patriots disguised themselves as Indians and boarded three British ships, loaded with tea, in Boston Harbor. They dumped all the tea overboard! That act is known as the Boston Tea Party. It sent the British a message: No taxes without our permission!

Two years later, in 1775, Paul Revere made his famous midnight ride. The Patriots had stored ammunition at Concord, outside Boston. They feared that the British planned to raid the supplies. So they set up a

A Fine Craftsman

Paul Revere was a well-known silversmith. People from all of the American colonies visited his silver shop in Boston to buy the beautiful pieces that he made. This famous painting shows Revere holding one of his silver teapots.

warning system. If British soldiers set out for Concord by land, one lantern would be hung in the steeple of Boston's North Church. If the British came by sea, two lanterns would be placed there. It would be Revere's job to spread the word so that the Patriot soldiers—the Minutemen—would be ready.

Dressed as an Indian, Paul Revere took part in the Boston Tea Party.

On the night of April 18, two lanterns were hung in the steeple. Revere set out for Concord on horseback. In each village he passed through, he woke up the Minutemen—crying "The British are coming!" At Lexington two other riders joined him. Then, a few miles from Concord, British soldiers arrested him. But one of the other riders galloped on to warn the Patriots. The British had no idea what Revere was up to, so they soon let him go.

The next day, British troops marched into Lexington and Concord. Thanks to Paul Revere, the Minutemen were ready. Shots were fired. The American Revolution—the war that gave freedom and independence to the United States—had begun!

Paul Revere's ride became famous. As the poem says:

In the hour of darkness and peril and need,

The people will waken and listen to hear

The hurrying hoof-beats of that steed,

And the midnight message of Paul Revere.

Sybil Ludington's Famous Ride

Paul Revere wasn't the only one who made a heroic nighttime ride during the American Revolution. Sybil Ludington rode twice as far as Revere—and she was only 16!

Sybil made her famous ride in 1777, when British troops attacked Danbury, Connecticut. Her father, Colonel Henry Ludington, commanded American troops in nearby New York. When he heard of the attack, he sent his daughter to round up his soldiers.

Sybil rode through the night of April 26. She covered 40 miles on dark roads and lanes, and alerted the soldiers. They didn't get to Danbury in time to stop the British from burning the town. But they later took part in a successful battle against the British.

Let's Bag It!

Do you have the perfect gift for someone? Then give it in a perfect bag that you can make yourself!

Begin with a bright, colorful bag—and lots of imagination. Decorate the bag with designs that you cut out from construction paper.

You can also use tissue paper, stickers, ribbons, glitter paint, and other materials. Use colored markers for details such as eyes and whiskers.

You can even match the design to the gift. If your gift is something to take to the beach, decorate the bag with a sailboat and the sun. If the gift is a bunch of daisies, use lots of colorful flowers on the bag. If it's for Valentine's Day, cover the bag with hearts. For an extra-special touch, make a greeting card that matches the bag!

Mickey the Dragon Slayer?

Mickey Mouse whistled as he drove. It was a fine, windy day for a traveling organ player and music teacher.

Around the bend, the wind grew even stronger. Mickey held onto his hat. Leaves, twigs, and straw swirled around his wagon.

As he drove by an open field, Mickey saw Goofy trying to fly a kite in the strong wind. "Hello!" Mickey cheerfully called. Goofy, struggling to keep his feet on the ground, was too busy to answer. Parents and disappointed children were hurrying away with their kites at their sides. "Golly! It's even too windy to fly a kite," Mickey said to himself, still holding onto his hat.

Mickey drove past a pond. "Wak!" Donald squawked angrily. "Wak! Wak!" The wind was causing problems here, too. Mickey saw that Donald was struggling to gather up the toy boats on his pond—before the wind broke them. He was trying to return the sailboats to their owners so they could get them safely home.

The wind blew and blew. As Mickey got closer to town, a poster blew off a pole right into his face. Mickey didn't have a chance to read what the poster said: "Wanted: Hero to Slay Windy Dragon."

Just then, the Mayor rushed up. "At last you're here!" he
cried.

Mickey was surprised. "What a warm welcome for a traveling—"

The Mayor interrupted. "You're just what we need, Mister
Dragon Slayer! But before you go to work, you'll want a fine
meal. Come along to Miss Minnie's."

"Dragon slayer?" Mickey gulped. "What does he mean?"

As the Mayor climbed up to drive the wagon, Mickey read the
poster that he had peeled off his face. But before he could
explain that there had been a mistake, the Mayor said, "Here
we are! Miss Minnie will take real good care of you." And the
Mayor rushed away.

"But . . ." Mickey began. Then he saw Miss Minnie and he couldn't say another word. Mickey was in love.

Miss Minnie said shyly, "Welcome, Mickey. We're so glad you've come to slay the dragon."

"But I'm not a dragon slayer," Mickey told her. He pointed to the sign on his wagon. Then Mickey saw the trick the wind had played with his sign. A twig had blown onto the letter "O," and the letter "P" had broken. Now the words were not quite the same. "Organ Player" had become "Drgan Slayer"! Uh-oh!

Goofy and Donald rushed up to Mickey and Miss Minnie.
"Garwsh," said Goofy, "it's a real honor to meet an honest-to-
goodness dragon slayer! If you slay that Windy Dragon, *Goofy's
Ye Olde Go Fly a Kite* business will really take off!"

"Hmmmph," snorted Donald. "You don't look like a dragon
slayer to me. But if you are, it will be smooth sailing for
*Donald's Ye Olde Go Float a
Sailboat.*"

"Good luck, Mister Dragon
Slayer! The whole town is
counting on you!" Goofy called
as he and Donald left.

What could Mickey do? He followed Miss Minnie into her Bake Shoppe, hoping to think of something—anything.

But even Miss Minnie's most delicious muffins didn't give him any ideas. Not knowing what else to do, Mickey got onto his wagon and drove out of town into the wind. The whole town cheered and waved him on his way. Mickey put on a brave smile and waved back. Only Miss Minnie knew the sad truth. But she waved and blew him a kiss. Mickey hoped she would understand when he came back without having slain the dragon—*if* he came back.

Mickey drove into the wind toward the hills. It was slow going. Then, suddenly, the wind stopped. Mickey stopped, too. "What happened to the wind?" he wondered. "I don't see anything. I don't hear anything. And I don't know what to do next!" So Mickey did what he always did when he didn't know what to do. He took out his flute, sat down, and began to play.

After playing several tunes, Mickey sensed he wasn't alone. Still playing, he slowly turned around. Standing there was a not very large, but definitely very curious dragon.

"Oh!" said Mickey. "You must be the Windy Dragon."

The dragon nodded and sighed sadly. The force of his sigh knocked Mickey over.

"Wow! It must be hard to make friends if you blow them over!" Mickey said.

The dragon nodded again, and helped Mickey up.

"Oh, that's okay," Mickey said. He felt sorry for the dragon. "I wish there was something I could do to help."

The dragon pointed to the flute, and he gestured for Mickey to play.

Mickey played a sad tune and saw a tear roll down the dragon's cheek. "Bet you're awfully lonely," Mickey said. "When I feel lonely, I play music. It cheers me up."

Then Mickey had an idea. "Maybe I could teach you to play music! Would you like that?"

The dragon nodded. Mickey gave him the flute and showed him how to blow into it. Smash! The force of the dragon's breath shattered the small instrument. The dragon looked even sadder.

"Hmm," said Mickey, thinking. "I know!" He took an extra organ pipe out of the wagon and carved some dragon-size finger holes in it. "Here we are—a dragon-strong flute!"

Mickey was a good music teacher, as well as an organ player. In a few hours, the dragon had learned to control his breath and play his special dragon-strong flute. By evening, the dragon and Mickey—who also had a new flute—were playing duets. They sounded great!

Mickey drove back to town with the dragon hiding inside his wagon. He arrived in the town square to cheers and welcomes from everyone.

Mickey held up his hands and the crowd quieted down.

"There's someone I'd like you all to meet," he said. Mickey opened the curtain, and out stepped the dragon. The townspeople drew back in horror. "This is the Windy Dragon," Mickey said. "He and I would like to play for you." Together, Mickey and Windy played and played.

"Hey, they're really good!" said the banker.

"Cool!" said the iceman, dancing with the greengrocer.

Then Mickey explained that Windy had learned to control his windy breath by playing music.

"Gawrsh, does that mean Windy could make a nice steady breeze to fly kites?" asked Goofy. "If he can, he's got a job at *Goofy's Ye Olde Go Fly a Kite*!"

Windy nodded yes, and he and Goofy shook hands.

"Hmm, could Windy make a gentle breeze to sail toy boats?" asked Donald.

"If he can, he can work for me at *Donald's Ye Olde Go Float a Sailboat* pond."

Windy nodded yes again, and shook Donald's hand.

Miss Minnie added, "Windy, if you have some time, could you come by the Bake Shoppe on baking day and stoke the oven?" Windy nodded yes

again and again. Miss Minnie hugged the dragon. Then she hugged and kissed Mickey, and the crowd cheered.

The Mayor said, "Mickey, we had no idea you were a dragon slayer and a music teacher!"

Mickey laughed. Then he pulled the stuck twig out of the "O" on the sign on his wagon, and fixed the broken "P." "To tell the truth," he said, "I never was a dragon slayer—just a traveling organ player and music teacher."

"I'm so glad," said the Mayor, who was also the schoolteacher. "I was afraid you were just a bad speller!"

Sea stars come in many different colors. With its bright spots, the **candy-cane star** is one of the most colorful sea stars of all. It lives in the Red Sea, in Egypt.

Most sea stars have five arms. But this one is different. It has 13 arms! With its orange color and many arms, it looks like a picture of the sun. That's why it's called the **spiny sun star**.

Stars of the Sea

There are stars in the sky . . . and stars in the ocean! Sea stars are found in oceans all over the world. They are sometimes called starfish—but they aren't fish. They belong to a group of animals called echinoderms (uh-KEE-no-durms). "Echinoderm" means "spiny-skinned"—and sea stars are covered with little spines.

The **blue sea star** is at home in the coral reefs of the Solomon Islands. Like the blue sea star, most sea stars prefer warm, shallow waters. But some live in cold waters, and some live at the bottom of the sea.

The **pincushion sea star** doesn't look much like other sea stars. But it still has five puffy arms spreading out from the center. This sea star lives in the Coral Sea, off the coast of Australia.

A sea star's body parts are all arranged in a balanced way. Its arms are all the same, and they all grow out from the center of its body. Can you guess what's at the tip of each arm? An eye!

On the undersides of the arms are hundreds of tiny tube feet. Each foot has a tiny suction cup. The sea star roams the ocean bottom looking for clams and other shellfish. When it finds a tasty clam, the sea star wraps its arms around its prey and uses its suction feet to force the shell open. Dinner is served!

A Walk Through Time

From sandals to sneakers, people have been wearing shoes for thousands of years.

What kind of shoes are you wearing? Sneakers? Party shoes? Sandals? Whatever you have on, you're walking around on a bit of history. That's because people have been wearing shoes for thousands of years!

Shoes are very important. Most animals have fur, thick pads, or hooves to protect their feet. You don't. Instead, it's your shoes that protect your feet from rough ground, hot pavement, and cold, wet weather.

This sandal is made from plant leaves. It is more than 8,000 years old.

The first shoes were probably sandals. Scientists recently found a bunch of prehistoric sandals in a cave in Missouri. The sandals are more than 8,000 years old! Many of the sandals were woven from plant leaves. A few were made from leather.

Ancient peoples in other parts of the world wore sandals, too. Most ancient Egyptians made sandals from papyrus. Papyrus is a reed that grows in the Nile River. But Egyptian rulers wore sandals made of fine leather. And their sandals were richly decorated.

As time went by, shoe styles changed. In the Middle Ages, European men wore cloth or leather shoes with long, pointed toes. The fad spread, and the toes became longer and longer. Some were 2 feet long! To keep from tripping, men fastened the toes to their knees with gold chains.

Women also had some strange shoe styles. In the 1500's, women wore shoes that were raised high above the ground. They were called platform

The rulers of ancient Egypt wore richly decorated sandals.

sandals. Some of them were 18 inches tall! It was impossible to walk in these shoes. The women had to lean on their servants' shoulders for support.

An Italian shoemaker came to their rescue. He invented a shoe in which just the heel, and not the whole shoe, was high.

This red velvet platform sandal was worn in the 1500's.

Women could walk in these high-heeled shoes—but it still wasn't easy!

In France, men also wore high-heeled shoes. The French King Louis XIV, who ruled in the 1600's, was only 5 feet, 3 inches tall. He was thrilled with the cork heels on his shoes that made him 5 inches taller!

For hundreds of years, the shoes of wealthy

King Louis XIV of France wore high-heeled shoes because they made him look taller.

Embroidered flowers decorate this pair of women's shoes from the 1800's.

women were made of delicate fabrics that were trimmed with ribbons and lace. Often, the shoes were uncomfortably tight. Women wore tight shoes to show that they had tiny, delicate feet.

In China, people also thought small feet were beautiful. This idea caused women a lot of pain. Until the early 1900's, the feet of upper-class Chinese girls were bound tightly in cloth bandages—causing the bones in their feet to stop growing.

One, Two, Buckle My Shoe

Over the years, people have thought up lots of different ways to keep their shoes on. Early sandals were tied on with straps that circled the feet.

Buckles were fashionable in the 1700's. Sometimes they were studded with diamonds. Then shoelaces became popular. Thomas Jefferson saw shoelaces being used in France. He liked them so much, he brought them to America.

In the 1800's, women wore high-button shoes. Each shoe had as many as 20 tiny buttons on it. Women used a special tool, a buttonhook, to fasten them. Even so, it seemed to take forever!

Today's shoes are much easier to put on. Besides laces, shoes and boots have zippers and hook-and-loop fasteners (Velcro).

Soft lily-foot slippers were worn by women in China to protect their painfully tiny feet.

When the girls became adults, they had oddly shaped, child-size feet. They were barely able to walk. They covered their feet with soft embroidered cloth shoes called lily-foot slippers.

Around the world, the 1800's and 1900's brought many changes to footwear. The sewing machine was invented, and shoes began to be made in factories. Now many more people could afford them.

Dorothy's Ruby Slippers

What are the most famous shoes in the world? Probably the ruby slippers in the 1939 movie *The Wizard of Oz*. Judy Garland wore them when she played Dorothy. The shoes are covered with sparkly, ruby-colored sequins. In the movie, they had magical powers that kept Dorothy safe from the Wicked Witch of the West!

Another important change was the idea of a right shoe and a left shoe. Before this change, both shoes in a pair were identical. People could wear either shoe on either foot!

Happy feet! No shoe has ever been more comfortable than the sneaker!

Dozens of shoe styles have come and gone in modern times. Toes have been round, square, and pointed. Women's shoes have had block heels, spike heels, and flat heels. And platform shoes are popular again.

What will be next? Whatever styles catch on, new shoes will help you put your best foot forward.

THE JOKE'S ON YOU!

What is a skunk's favorite food?

A peanut butter and smelly sandwich!

What do you call a fish without an eye?

A fsh!

Name five things that contain milk.

Ice cream, cheese, and three cows.

What are the dirtiest rabbits in the world?

Dust bunnies!

Why did the farmer drive a steamroller over his vegetables?

He forgot to plant squash!

What is smarter than a talking parrot?

A spelling bee!

What would the world be like without Winnie the Pooh?

Un-bear-able!